Wonders

Mc
Graw
Hill
Education

A

Program Authors

Diane August

Donald R. Bear

Janice A. Dole

Jana Echevarria

Douglas Fisher

David Francis

Vicki Gibson

Jan Hasbrouck

Margaret Kilgo

Jay McTighe

Scott G. Paris

Timothy Shanahan

Josefina V. Tinajero

McGraw Hill Education

UNIT
2

THE BIG CONCEPT

Our Community

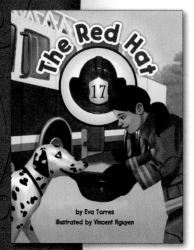

WEEK I JOBS AROUND TOWN   SOCIAL STUDIES

The Red Hat Realistic Fiction 6
by Eva Torres; illustrated by Vincent Nguyen

Read Together Firefighters at Work Nonfiction 22

WEEK 2 BUILDINGS ALL AROUND SOCIAL STUDIES

The Pigs, the Wolf, and the Mud Fantasy 26
by Ellen Tarlow; illustrated by Pablo Bernasconi

Read Together Homes Around the World Nonfiction . . 44

Go Digital! http://connected.mcgraw-hill.com/

WEEK 3 A COMMUNITY IN NATURE   SCIENCE

At a Pond Nonfiction 48

by Nancy Finton

(Read Together) **Way Down Deep** Poetry 62

by Mary Ann Hoberman

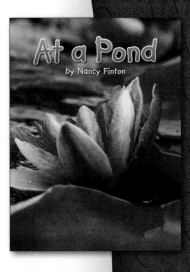

WEEK 4 LET'S HELP   SOCIAL STUDIES

Nell's Books Fantasy 64

by Miriam Cohen; illustrated by Emilie Chollat

(Read Together) **Kids Can Help!** Nonfiction 82

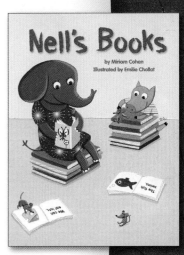

WEEK 5 FOLLOW THE MAP   SOCIAL STUDIES

(Read Together) **Fun with Maps** Nonfiction 86

(Read Together) **North, East, South, or West?**

Nonfiction 94

Glossary 96

Essential Question

What jobs need to be done in a community?

Read about a firefighter's exciting job.

Go Digital!

The Red Hat

by Eva Torres

illustrated by Vincent Nguyen

Jen has a **new** job.
She gets a red hat.

She will **use** this hat a lot.

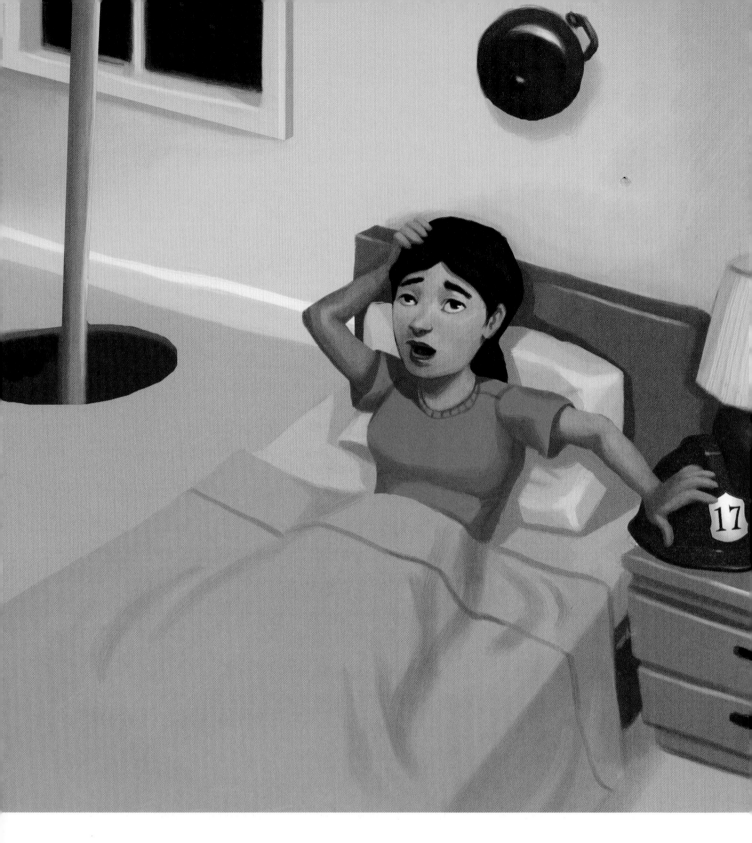

Jen is in bed.

There is a bell!

She grabs the red hat.

Jen can get down like this.
Go, Jen, go!

Jen hops on.
Go, Jen, go!

It is a big fire!
Jen can **help**.

The fire is out.

Jen is wet.

Thank you, Jen!

Jen plays with Matt and Jill.
There is a bell **again**.

Jen gets the red hat.
She gets in the truck.
Go, Jen, go!

Rex is up there.

He will not come to Jim.

Jen will help!

Jen gets Rex.

Jim is glad.

Rex is glad, too.

He has a new red bed.

Thank you, Jen!

Meet the Illustrator

Vincent Nguyen says, "I live near a firehouse in New York City, so I'm familiar with its sights and sounds. To illustrate *The Red Hat,* I just walked around the block and took photos that helped me draw the pictures."

Illustrator's Purpose

Vincent Nguyen wanted to show what the inside of a firehouse looks like. Draw something that is inside a firehouse. Label your picture.

©Vincent Nguyen

Respond to the Text

Retell

Use your own words to retell *The Red Hat*. Tell who the characters are, where they are, and what happens to them.

Character	Setting	Events

Write

Would you like to have Jen's job? Describe what you would like or not like, and why. Use these sentence starters:

I think Jen's job is...
I would like...

Make Connections
COLLABORATE

 How does Jen help her community?
ESSENTIAL QUESTION

Compare Texts

Read about what real firefighters do.

hat

boots   pole

Firefighters at Work

A bell rings at the firehouse.
Firefighters slide down a pole.
They put on special clothes fast!

Richard Hutchings/PhotoEdit

22

The firefighters jump in a fire truck.
The red truck speeds to the fire.
It has a loud **siren** and a flashing red
light. That tells cars to move away!

lights

ladder

hose

The brave firefighters get to work.
They use hoses to spray water.
Their special clothes **protect** them.
They put out the fire!

Now it is time for lunch.

They have lunch together.

Then they wait for the next bell.

Make Connections

How do firefighters help the community?

Essential Question

The Pigs, the Wolf, and the Mud

by Ellen Tarlow

illustrated by
Pablo Bernasconi

Three pigs **lived** in a mud hut.

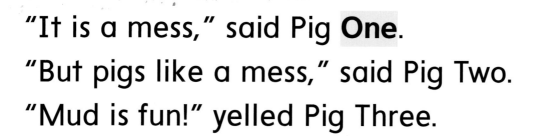

"It is a mess," said Pig **One**.

"But pigs like a mess," said Pig Two.

"Mud is fun!" yelled Pig Three.

"Get this!" yelled Pig One.
She tossed mud to Pig Two.
"Mud is fun!" yelled Pig Three.

The bell rang.

"Little pigs, pigs, pigs, let me in."

31

"It is a big, bad wolf!" said Pig One.
"We can not let you in," yelled the
pigs. "You will eat us up."

"**Then** I will huff and puff,"
the wolf yelled back.
He huffed, huffed, huffed.
He puffed, puffed, puffed.

"Yuck!" said the wolf.
"I can not huff in mud.
I can not puff in mud."

He rang the bell again.
"Pigs, pigs, pigs, let me in!"
he yelled.
"We will not let you in!"
the pigs yelled back.

"Then I will kick, kick, kick,"
said the wolf.
He kicked, kicked, kicked.

36

The hut fell in!

"Yuck!" said the wolf.

"I can not look at this mud."

"You pigs are a big mess!"
"Yes!" yelled the pigs.
"Pigs like a big mess!"

"But I do not!" yelled the
wolf. "I must get this mud
off. Good-bye, pigs."

"Let's make a hut," said Pig One.

"We **could** use bricks," said Pig Two.

"We could use sticks," said Pig Three.

40

"We will use mud," said Pig One.
"Mud is good!" said Pig Two.
"Mud is fun!" yelled Pig Three.
"Yuck!" said the wolf.

Meet the Illustrator

Pablo Bernasconi loves illustrating animals doing funny things. Pablo's studio is a mess, full of junk and papers. But Pablo loves being surrounded by his things, just as the pigs in the story love being surrounded by mud.

Pablo Bernasconi

Illustrator's Purpose

Pablo Bernasconi likes to draw funny animals. Draw and write about an animal doing something you think is funny.

42

Respond to the Text

Retell

Use your own words to retell important events in *The Pigs, the Wolf, and the Mud.*

Character	Setting	Events

Write

Look at pages 40 to 41. The pigs need a plan. Write directions for the pigs to follow when building their hut. Use these sentence starters:

First, the pigs need to...
Next, they can...
Then, they can...

Make Connections

COLLABORATE

How is the pigs' hut like a building you know? How is it different?

ESSENTIAL QUESTION

Read Together

Compare Texts

Read about the different homes people make.

Homes Around the World

There are many kinds of **homes**. People **build** their homes to fit the place they live!

This home is built into a rock.

This home is made of wood.

This is a good home for a wet place. There is a lot of water here. The stilts help keep this home dry.

This is a good home for a hot place.
There is a lot of clay in this place.
People use it to build homes. Clay
keeps the home cool inside.

**This home is
made of clay.**

An igloo is made of ice.

There is a lot of ice in this place. People can use it to build. This is an igloo. People don't live in igloos. But they are good **shelter** from the cold.

What is your home like?

Make Connections

Which home do you think the pigs in *The Pigs, the Wolf, and the Mud* would like? Why? **Essential Question**

Essential Question

Where do animals live together?

Read about animals that live at a pond.

Go Digital!

At a Pond

by Nancy Finton

Who lives at a pond?

Who is **under** the water?
Who is on the land?
Who can fly to the pond?
Let's see!

Frogs live at a pond.

They swim and hop and jump.

Frogs rest on plants on the pond.

This frog is hunting for bugs.

It sees a bug.

Will it get a snack?

It has to be quick! Yum, yum!

(inset) David & Micha Sheldon / FI Online/ Photolibrary; Nigel Dennis/Gallo Images/SuperStock

Ducks come to the pond.

They **eat** lots **of** bugs and plants.

This duck dips its bill to get bugs.

Dip, dip, dip!

54

Ducks make nests on land.
They use twigs and grass.
Who is in the eggs?
Quack, quack, quack!

Turtles can be on land and in water.
They swim and swim.
Then they stop and rest in the sun.

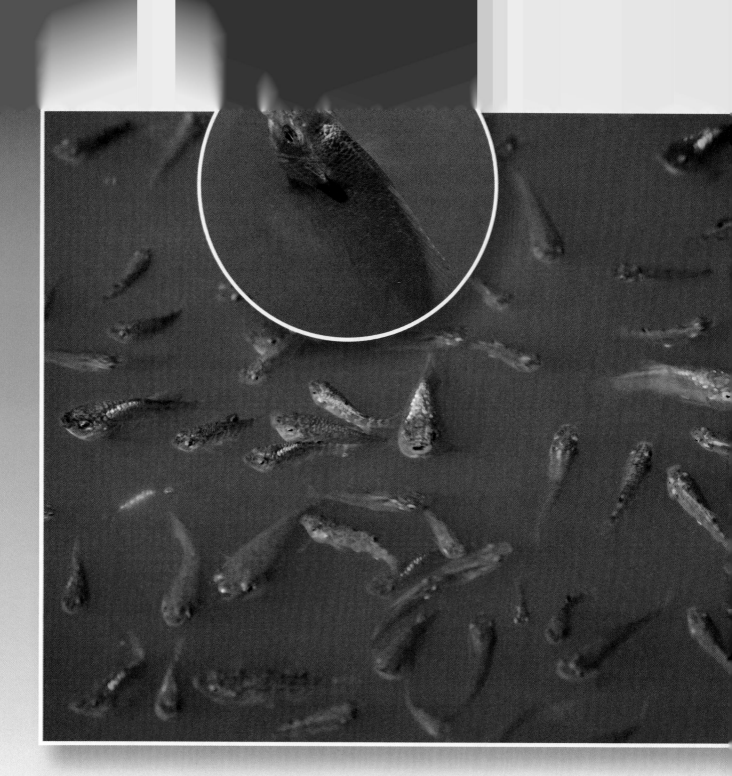

Can fish be on land? **No!**

Fish live in water.

They swim, swim, swim.

A big fish comes up to eat. Gulp!

Bugs like water.

Lots of bugs live at a pond.

A dragonfly is a big bug.

You can see it at a pond.

egret

raccoon

newt

goldfish

toad

beaver

Look at the animals at a pond.
Who are they?

Meet the Author

Nancy Finton says, "I love living and working in a big, busy city. But sometimes it feels too big and busy! Then I wish I were sitting by a quiet pond with the frogs and turtles."

Author's Purpose

Nancy Finton wanted to write about animals that live at a pond. She wanted readers to see the animals close up. Draw a place where animals live together. Write about your picture.

Respond to the Text

Retell

Use your own words to retell three important details in *At a Pond*.

Main Topic		
Detail	Detail	Detail

Write

Write two more pages about one of the animals in *At a Pond*. Use the photos to help you. Use these sentence starters:

This animal lives. . .
This animal can. . .

Make Connections

COLLABORATE

How is the pond like the bayou in *Babies in the Bayou?*

ESSENTIAL QUESTION

(br) Lisa Stokes/Flickr/Getty Images

Read Together

Compare Texts

Read about animals that live in the water.

Way Down Deep

by Mary Ann Hoberman

Underneath the water
Way down deep
In sand and stones and seaweed
Starfish creep
Snails inch slowly
Oysters sleep
Underneath the water
Way down deep.

Make Connections

? How is under the sea like the pond? How is it different? **Essential Question**

Essential Question

How do people help out in the community?

Read about an elephant who loves books.

Go Digital!

The sun is hot.

Pig is big.

Nell's Books

by Miriam Cohen

Illustrated by Emilie Chollat

We can eat lots.

The fish swims.

Nell liked to read.

She liked it a lot.

Nell could sit and read **all day** long.

"Will you play with us, Nell?"
called Cat and Dog.
"Shh!" said Nell. "I am reading."

"Will you shop with me, Nell?"
asked Pig.
"Shh!" said Nell. "This is good!"

"That Nell is not fun at all,"
said Dog.
"She just reads," said Cat.
"She will not do a thing!"

Then one day it rained.
Dog and Cat set up a tent.
Pig got dressed up for fun.
"This is good," said Dog.
"Yes!" said Pig and Cat.

It rained the next day, too.

"We **want** to go out," said Dog.

"We are sick of tents and dressing up,"
said Pig and Cat.

Nell went to **her** shelf.
"Here, Dog," she said.
"I think you will like this."
"Yuck!" said Dog.

"This will be fun for Pig," said Nell.

"Cat, you will like this a lot."

"Ick!" said Cat and Pig.

"Shh!" said Nell. "Let's read."

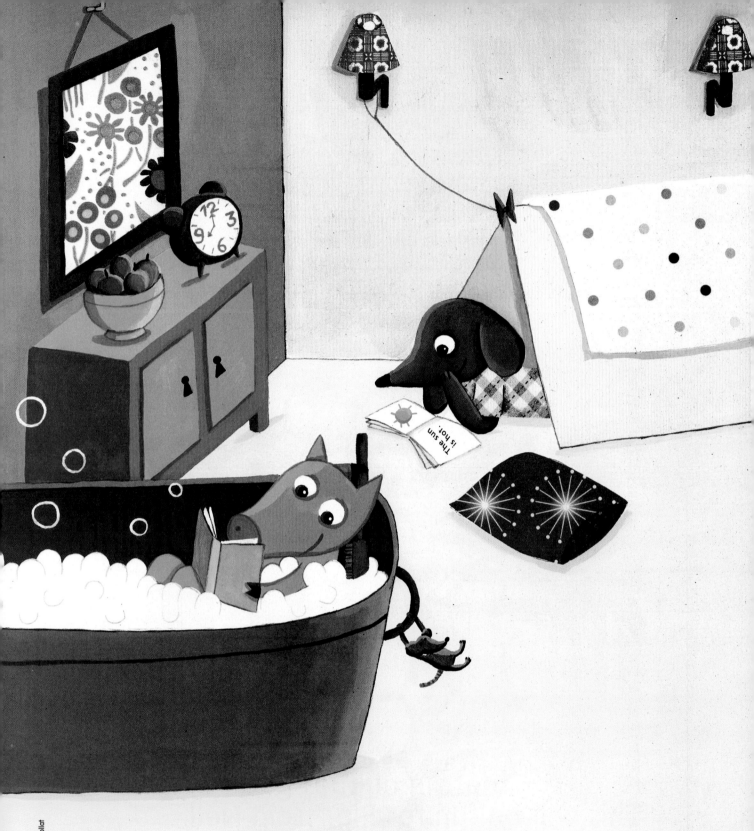

Dog read in his tent.
Pig read in a tub.
Cat read in a pot.

They read all day long.
"This is fun!" said Cat
and Dog and Pig.

The next day, Nell heard clanging.
She heard banging.
"Nell, come quick!" called Dog.

"We did this for you," said Dog.
"You can hand out books to all,"
said Cat.
"Nell is good at that," said Pig.
"That is just my wish!" said Nell.

Nell got in.
"Let's hand out books," she said.

"Shh!" said Dog and Cat and Pig.
"Let us read!"

Meet the Author

Miriam Cohen says, "I have always loved elephants because they are smart animals that do nice things for other elephants. I imagined an elephant that was so smart she could read. I had fun writing about how she shared her love of books with her friends."

Author's Purpose

Miriam Cohen wanted to tell about an animal that helps its community. Draw an animal helping its community. Write about it.

Miriam Cohen

80

Respond to the Text

Retell

Use your own words to retell important events in *Nell's Books.*

Character	Setting	Events

Write

Use *Nell's Books* as a model to write a fantasy about a character who helps. Use these sentence starters:

My character likes to. . .
My character helps when. . .

Make Connections
COLLABORATE

? How does giving books out help a community?

ESSENTIAL QUESTION

Read
Together

Compare Texts

Read about how kids can
help out.

Kids Can Help!

How can kids help the **neighborhood**?

Kids can help grow a **garden**! It is fun
to plant seeds and help them grow.

A community garden is a great place to help. The plants are pretty to look at. And everyone can enjoy fresh fruits and vegetables.

Kids can help clean the playground. They can pick up trash. They can **recycle** cans and bottles.

Recycling makes the neighborhood clean. Recycling helps our Earth, too.

Do you want to help your neighborhood? Think about what you can do.

How We Can Help

1. Plant a garden.

2. Clean the playground.

3. Recycle cans and bottles.

Make Connections

How does a garden help a community? **Essential Question**

Read Together

Essential Question

How can you find your way around?

Learn how to use a map.

Go Digital!

A map is a drawing of a **place**.

A map shows us where we are.

It shows us how to get **around**, too.

Phil's Room

A map can be of a small place.

This is a map of Phil's room.

How **many** windows do you see?

What is next to Phil's bed?

What is **by** the door?

A map can be of a big place.
This is a map of a town.
What places do you see on
the map?

88

Which street is the market on?

What is by the firehouse?

How would you **walk** from the school to the library?

A map can be of a fun place.
This is a map of a park.
The symbols on maps stand for real
things. On this map,  stands for
a place to eat lunch.

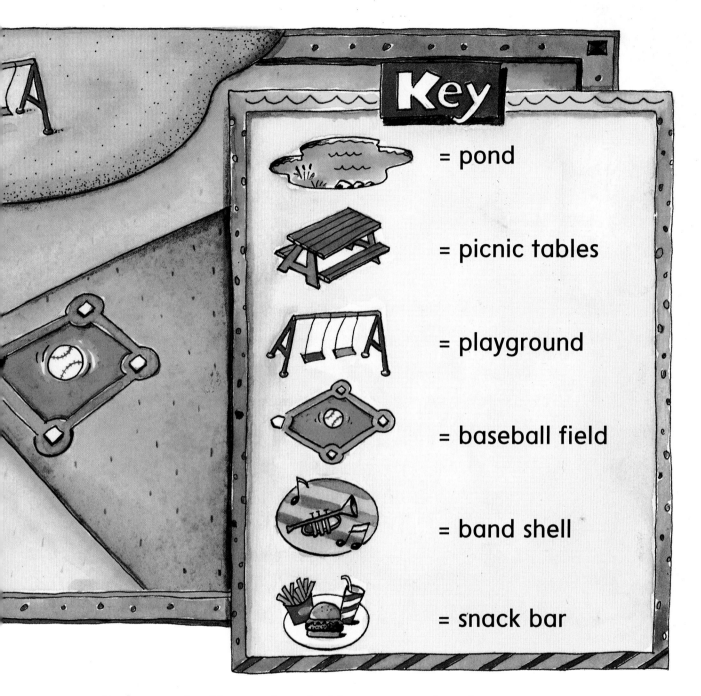

= pond

= picnic tables

= playground

= baseball field

= band shell

= snack bar

A key tells what the symbols mean.
Match the symbol in the key with
the one on the map.
What symbol stands for the pond?
What does 🛝 stand for?

A map can be of an imaginary place.
This is a treasure map.
What routes could you take to get
to the chest of gold? This map could
help you a lot!

Key

 = pirate ship

= cave

 = waterfall

= volcano

= cove

✖ = chest of gold

Respond to the Text

1. Use detail from the selection to summarize. SUMMARIZE

2. Why does the author show different kinds of maps? What does this help us to understand about maps? WRITE

3. How could the map of the park help you? TEXT TO WORLD

Genre Nonfiction

Compare Texts
Read about the
directions on a map.

Read
Together

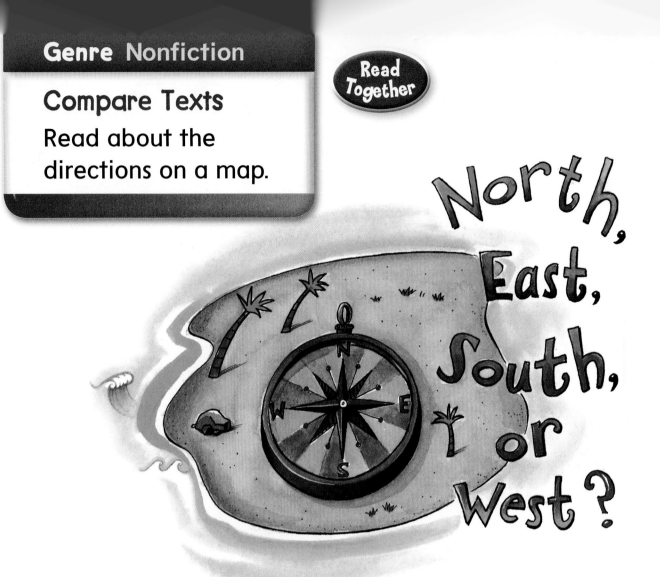

North,
East,
South,
or
West?

Many maps show directions. North,
East, South, and West are directions.
Directions tell us which way to go.

Look at the map of the zoo. Find
each direction. Is the lion north
or south of the snack bar? Are the
chimps closer to the east or west?

Illustration: Steven Mach

94

Make Connections

? What is north of the baseball field on the map of Bell Park?

Essential Question

Glossary

What is a Glossary? A glossary can help you find the meanings of words. The words are listed in alphabetical order. You can look up a word and read it in a sentence. Sometimes there is a picture to help you.

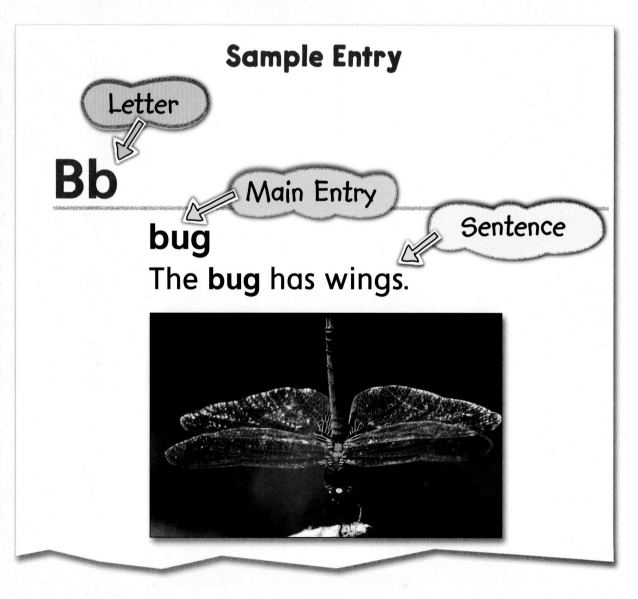

Sample Entry

Letter

Bb

Main Entry

Sentence

bug

The **bug** has wings.

Bb

book
It is good to read a **book**.

bug
The **bug** has wings.

97

Ee

eat

Jess can **eat** an apple.

Jj

job

A vet has a fun **job**.

Ll

lunch

This is a good **lunch**.

Mm

mess

This room is a **mess**.

(t) Jupiterimages/Comstock Images/Getty Images; (b) Ash Lindsey Photography/Flickr/Getty Images

mud

The pigs are in the **mud**.

Nn

new

Jim is getting **new** shoes.

Pp

pond
Ducks swim in the **pond**.

Rr

red
The truck is **red**.

Ss

shelf

The books are on the **shelf**.

Tt

tent

We can sleep in a **tent**.

three
Three frogs sit.

Ww

walk
The friends **walk** together.

(t) IT Stock/PunchStock; (b) Ariel Skelley/Blend Images LLC